THE GOSPEL OF

SE~~X~~

DATING, RELATING, AND MATING

THE GOSPEL OF
SEX
DATING, RELATING, AND MATING

Dustin Hall

Remnant
Publications
COLDWATER MI

Published by
Remnant Publications
649 East Chicago Road
Coldwater MI 49036
517-279-1304
www.remnantpublications.com

All Bible quotations are taken from the
English Standard Version unless otherwise noted.

The author assumes responsibility for
the accuracy of all footnotes and references.

Cover designed by Penny Hall
Text edited by Anthony Lester
Text designed by Greg Solie • Altamont Graphics

ISBN 1-933291-03-6

TABLE OF CONTENTS

INTRODUCTION

Yeah, it's a cliché. But I am a Bible-believing Christian, meaning I believe in the Bible's truth and accuracy in all points on which it touches. For this I am not embarrassed and make no apologies, and you shouldn't either, because its clear message offers the only hope for every soul in such uncertain times.

Now God has shown great mercy on me, granting me victory over temptations as I surrender to His will. But more than that, He has offered forgiveness when I have stumbled and fallen. So no, I'm not writing to you as someone who boasts that I'm without sin—who is above experiencing trials and tribulations. Quite the contrary.

Yet I thank God that He chooses sinners like me, to share His good news to a sin-darkened world. And in this case, I believe He has chosen me to be a trumpet-like voice on the issue of sexual purity in the lives of young people. My constant prayer during the writing of this book was that He would hide me behind His cross so that the words written herein would not be mine, but His. That way, you and I are both getting a benefit.

Hearing the Lord's Voice

As much as I would like to give an in-depth personal testimony about how God has led in my life, for the sake of brevity, I will only share the portion of my story that deals directly with the topic of sexual purity and how I came to write this book.

A few years ago, as the pastor of a new church, I needed to provide a little more for my family financially. I took a peculiar and challenging position with a local non-profit organization: developing a sexual-abstinence curriculum and seminar for public schools.

Frankly, I began this job a little overwhelmed. You know the state of schools today; how easy could it be to present a no-sex-until-marriage message to a secular audience bombarded with a casual-sex culture?

I felt like a second grader staring at calculus equations! I didn't know what direction to take, or how and what to present to these young, easily-influenced minds. Yet after much prayer, I knew this was God's will. I set out on the task in faith, with prayer and study, and soon He gave me a powerful purpose, vision, and passion for this project. He made the way I should go crystal clear, parting the waters of the Jordan as I faithfully stepped in.

Part of the challenge was that I myself had never heard a clear message on sexual purity from my own church. I had never heard a teacher or preacher or *anyone else* address God's will on this topic. Can you imagine the challenge? If our own church can't be an effective voice for abstinence in the body of believers, how could we expect to do that for others?

Indeed, Christianity as a whole has been hitting and missing on this topic for far too long. And it's getting much worse, as we'll discover together in this book. But that's why I'm writing—it is time for believers to make a stand and present the lifestyle that Christ wants all of us to live, including young people like you.

As we'll see, His will is abundantly clear on the issue of sex before marriage. Thus it is my hope that this book will be an empowering agent for change and a convicting vessel for young and old alike. We all need it.

What Exactly Is Sexual Abstinence?

The definition of sexual abstinence will likely vary depending on your dictionary. For the sake of clarity, I would like to define it simply as: to abstain from *all* sexual activity until marriage, *regardless of the past.*

The first part of this definition is a good overview of the biblical stance of sexual activity, which enjoins us to "flee sexual immorality" (1 Corinthians 6:18). Yet my definition also speaks to the forgiving and restoring power of the Savior. Regardless of your past, you can make a decision to avoid all sexual activity before marriage. But also take note: I have placed an emphasis on *all* sexual activity, which includes activities that many people believe do not affect their purity or virginity. (This topic will be discussed in detail later.)

An Overview

This book is not a sexual education resource: It does not discuss anatomy. It's not a scare tactic either: It does not offer up graphic descriptions or pictures of sexually transmitted diseases. In some cases, of course, facts and statistics are necessary. You'll find relevant data regarding the media, sexual issues in teen culture, and the epidemic of STDs.

But the thrust of this book is to help all Christians become "children of light" (Ephesians 5:8). It's a wake-up call, yes, but a wake-up call that provides a positive and realistic view of biblical sexuality. It will help you find power and victory through the Lord to overcome temptation. You'll discover that sexual abstinence not only protects you from so many real dangers, but that it simply pleases God.

I'd like to call your attention to the chapter directed to parents, the last one in the book. It will greatly benefit the intended audience, but I think you can also gain insight from this section, so please read every chapter.

Finally, I believe that sex is a gift from God, given to His children in the Garden of Eden (Genesis 2:25, 4:1). Sex is a wonderful act that people can give to one another. So this book isn't a put down on sex. Sex isn't dirty; it is very good. Yet sex can only be truly good in the right context: marriage. Let's see how we can keep it that way in our lives.

CHAPTER ONE

The Good News
About Goals

Everyone has at least one goal or dream, regardless of who they are. It's not a matter of gender, religion, race, age, or anything other than one's humanity. If you're human, you have goals you'd like to accomplish. Those can be as short term as getting a good grade, buying a car, or getting a job. They can be as long term as owning a home or getting married. Yet even if you can't identify a specific goal, you probably have a picture in your head of what you want for your future.

Many know that to achieve their goals, they'll have to follow a certain path of success. Of course, some don't know what that specific path is just yet, but I imagine if you have a goal, you'll agree there is something you can do to increase your chances of realizing that goal.

As an example, say your goal is to be a doctor. To increase the odds of success, you'll have to stay in school, get into college, and manage your budget wisely. You might also choose to take on a marathon one day; to achieve that goal, you're going to have to train and eat well. But those are easy-to-see pathways.

What often isn't so easy to plan for is letting obstacles get in your way. Sometimes life throws you curve balls you can't dodge, like you get sick or a loved one dies. But sometimes what you do in just one area of your life will forever limit or restrain you from accomplishing your goals. I believe that we all have inside us what it takes to be successful, but that success all depends on our personal decisions. To be a doctor, you can't sit around and play video games all day. If you want to be a marathoner, you can't subsist on donuts for every meal.

And that's just it. The decisions you make every day will affect your future, possibly the rest of your life. I knew two young men who were killed in an auto accident because they were drunk. They died because of some very bad decisions they made that night. I don't know if the threat of danger even crossed their minds, but that's irrelevant now, isn't it?

Of course, not every decision will be as life altering as that, but it is a good yet extreme example of how important it is to consider the impact of even one decision on your goals.

A Better Goal

As Christians, you and I have another goal that non-believers do not have: heaven. We look forward to the day of living in eternity with Jesus, of playing in green fields with lions and singing with the angels on the glassy sea.

We also know that a major obstacle to achieving this goal has already been overcome. "For God so loved the world that He gave His only begotten Son, that whoever believes in Him should not perish but have everlasting life" (John 3:16). This ultimate good news verse says that although we deserve to perish, by God's Son we have the gift of eternal life.

But we have to be careful, because you can be sure that if you can make a decision that will affect the success of your goals here on earth, there are also things you can do to make reaching heaven that much more difficult.

Make no mistake, Christians can and do leave their heavenly dreams behind by making the decision to not follow Jesus, and instead follow their own desires. And I'm here to tell you that one of the most challenging decisions you'll be faced with that can easily become a major obstacle for your goals—earthly or heavenly—is whether or not to have sex before marriage.

I know. It seems like a startling scare tactic, right? Maybe, but it is also a clear fact. So you want to be a doctor? Let's talk about some earthly obstacles first: What potential obstacle to that goal could come from you having sex before marriage? Well, an unplanned pregnancy of course. Babies change everything—they require your energy, your time, and your money. The consequences of pregnancy, planned or not, are limitless! Try juggling medical school with a full-time job and providing care, shelter, and love for a baby. It could be more than you could endure and still achieve your dreams.

Another obvious consequence is disease. Sexually transmitted diseases (STDs) can result in a lot of medical costs, heartache and pain, worry and grief, and even embarrassment. You might be able to make it through medical school with an STD, but you can't underscore enough the emotional and physical obstacles you'll be forced to overcome along the way.

There are also deeply psychological issues that come with pre-marital sexual activity. When a person has sex, they basically give all of themselves over to another person—body, emotion, heart, and mind. Sex is *not* just about doing something that feels good in the short term. We aren't built that way, as we'll see in another chapter.

It always hurts more when sex is thrown into a relationship and the relationship fails. That kind of heartbreak is a plague, making your entire body ache and consuming your thoughts. It affects your life and is baggage you'll carry forever. This pain can result in long-term depression, anxiety, guilt, from which it can take years to recover. Some never do recover. Imagine dealing with that obstacle when studying for an exam.

Along these same lines, your social life can be affected. Gossip could be a problem, and your reputation can be ruined depending on the nature and outcome of the relationship. You might end up spending your focus on trying to restore friendships and trust, rather than writing that term paper or training for that marathon.

Dealing with Ultimate Reality

It's true that few people think of these things when they're in the heat of passion. But that's why I wrote this book. So you can think of these obstacles before getting yourself into a situation that you might end up regretting for the rest of your life. The only foolproof way to keep these kinds of obstacles from getting in the way of your goals here on earth is not to have premarital sex. Yes, it's really that simple.

When I was young, I thought I was invincible. I thought I would be taken care of no matter what happened to me. But I didn't realize there is a difference between having your needs met and being shielded from the consequences of your choices.

And God does allow His children to suffer the consequences of their decisions. This does not mean that God loves you any less or that He wants to see you suffer. If anything, He's trying to show you the price of rebellion so that you will avoid the same mistakes in the future. This is why many young people find themselves in terrible predicaments. We might cry out, "God, why are you doing this to me?" if we are faced with a pregnancy or an STD. But God has already tried to protect you—by giving you the freedom and option not to have sinful sex.

And with that, what about heaven? How can premarital sex keep you from reaching eternity? The Bible could not be clearer: Sexual activity of any kind before marriage is a sin (1 Corinthians 6:9). And sin is an obstacle to our relationship with God (Isaiah 59:1, 2).

If you choose a life of sin over a life in Jesus, you will not have a place in heaven. It sounds extreme, I know, but that's the plain truth. To discuss sexual activity before marriage without calling it a sin would be speaking in denial. (We'll go deeper into the evidence that premarital sex in sinful in the next chapter.)

If you are willing to sin, to have premarital sex, you are putting your selfish desires over true communion with God. If heaven is a place of eternal communion with the Lord, should we pursue something that would keep us from full communion with Him now?

Don't think I want to scare you into not having premarital sex. You should choose to keep yourself pure because you love God, but it's your decision. Yet it is time to be straightforward about a problem plaguing our church and affecting the eternal destinies of young people.

The fact is that with premarital sex, you set up limits to life on earth and build a wall to the heavenly goal we all share. The Christian life is about the blessed hope (Titus 2:13). Jesus has prepared you a mansion in heaven and will soon come to make eternity a reality (John 14:1–3). Will you let a here-and-now sexual obstacle come between you and Him? It's a decision you'll have to make.

Special Note: Have you already made that mistake of premarital sexual activity? Don't fear, because there is forgiveness (1 John 1:9). If you have chosen sex before marriage in the past over God's will, ask Jesus to forgive you and your sin will be cleansed. Stay with me, because we'll talk more about this in a later chapter.

☙

CHAPTER TWO

The Good News About Being the Light

Countless young people have asked me, "Where does it say in the Bible that sexual activity before marriage is sin?" Do you also want to know what the Bible really says about sexual purity? Look no further than the writings of the Apostle Paul. One of his goals was to eradicate sexual impurity from the early church.

In his day, sexual promiscuity was an accepted part of life. Indeed, it was not uncommon for professed believers to attend church, leave there, and have sex with someone other than their spouse that same day. And it wasn't merely accepted; it was promoted!

Paul directly challenges this behavior in the first chapter of Romans, but it is also a prevailing theme in most of his letters to the churches. But one particularly strident warning is found in the fifth chapter of Ephesians.

In verse 8, Paul writes, "For at one time you were darkness, but now you are light in the Lord. Walk as children of light." Paul speaks of a dramatic transformation in people who come to Christ: They were once darkness, but they are now light. (They don't have lights; instead, they are lights!) That's a high calling for Christians. But what does it have to do with sex before marriage? The idea of complete transformation is introduced to the church in Ephesus *during a discussion of sexual purity.*

How do we know? Because verses 3 to 5 deal with sexual perversity, setting the context for the rest of the chapter. Let's break down the chapters in this verse to examine the elicit set of behaviors that Paul condemns:

- **Sexual Immorality** (v. 3) – The Greek word is "Porneia," from which the English word "pornography" is derived. Paul uses this term whenever referring to sexual activity outside of marriage (1 Corinthians 6:9, 18). In some Bible translations, "immorality" is translated as "fornication."

- **Impurity** (v. 3) – Sexual impurity can include the perversions of thoughts, words, and feelings. Whereas fornication, or "immorality," is a physical act, impurity can include all forms of sexual sin, including thoughts.

- **Covetousness** (v. 3) – Although the adjective "sexual" is not used here, it is understood in context with the rest of the verse. Paul here is writing about coveting or desiring a person's body for sexual pleasure. In verse 5, Paul calls this behavior idolatry. Sexually objectifying someone else's body through lustful thoughts is an act of worship. Apparently lustful desires were driving the Ephesians to see people only as sexual objects. (Sounds a lot like today's culture, doesn't it?) Paul even goes as far to direct us to the second commandment (Exodus 20:4-6).

- **Foolish talk** (v. 4) – In context, "sexual" talk or "empty words" refers to any talk that is inappropriate, but particularly "filthy" subjects. Paul may have had more than just sexually driven talk in mind when using this phrase, but it fits in our study.

- **Sexual joking** (v. 4) – Paul tells people to not even speak or joke in a sexual manner, calling it filthiness.

- **Associate** (vs. 6, 7) – Associating with people who speak and use "empty words" or people that do not use reverent and appropriate language and have perverse opinions is as dangerous as committing the deed itself!

Paul has covered all the bases here, hasn't he? Sexual acts, impure thoughts, sexual joking and talk, coveting the body sexually, and associating with people who act and think in these ways. Then Paul pulls no punches—"For you may be sure of this, that everyone who is sexually immoral or impure, or who is covetous [that is an idolater] has no inheritance in the kingdom of Christ and of God. Let no one deceive you with empty words for because of these things the wrath of God comes upon the children of disobedience" (Ephesians 5:6, 7).

There you have it. Paul makes it plain: Sexual impurity will keep people out of the kingdom of heaven. It's a heavy, sobering thought for sure. But let's look a little deeper and apply Paul's message to today's culture. We'll repeat the previous list here, adjusting it for you and me.

- **Sexual Immorality** (v. 3) – *Any* sexual contact outside marriage is sinful. The only "pure sex" is sexual activity between a husband and wife. Many today might argue about pure sexual activities outside of marriage, but clearly Paul teaches there is no such thing.

- **Impurity** (v. 3) – Sexually impure thoughts, words, feelings, and actions are sinful and must be overcome by followers of Christ, like you and me.

- **Covetousness** (v. 3) – Any time a mind concentrates with lust on physical appearance, it is sin. Paul even calls it a form of false worship (idolatry). If our connection with God is interrupted by inappropriate sexual thoughts, our focus is no longer on Jesus. It has been redirected toward a person whom we have made into a sexual idol. This applies to everyday people and those we see in television, movies, and video games. It also applies to what we hear in music.

- **Sexual talk and joking** (v. 4) – All talk that involves sexually inappropriate themes, issues, or jokes are sinful. Dirty jokes and sexually driven words do not bring glory to God. Also consider the impressions you make on those who don't think like you. Would they be impressed with your behavior, or will they only remember your filthy speech?

- **Associate** (vs. 6, 7) – Associating with people who encourage impure thoughts, words, actions, etc., is dangerous. This means friends, yes, but also anything that touches our lives, like movies. When we listen to music, we are associating with the Rolling Stones or

50 Cent. When we play certain video games, we are associating with violence and illicit sex. How are we to keep our thoughts pure if we are associating with people and things that are impure? We cannot compromise on our associations!

Sexual perversion has been a nagging problem for God's people in the past. Sadly, it is no different today. You can easily find sexual impurity on television, on the internet, at the work place, and in our hearts. Yet we all must find a way to rid ourselves of this kind of sin, because it is getting in the way of our relationship with God.

Yet Ephesians not only points out the problem in no uncertain terms, it also gives us the solution! It begins in Ephesians 5:8: "For at one time you were darkness, but now you are light in the Lord. Walk as children of light." Paul calls Christians out of the behaviors that are impure, beseeching us to leave our lives of "darkness." Moreover, we are to be the opposite of dark; we are to be light. If darkness is sexual sin, then light must be sexual purity. If sexual sin is immorality, impurity, covetousness, dirty talk, and bad associations, we must turn our backs on those things if we seek to be in the kingdom of God.

But being a light extends to more than just going to heaven; it's also about helping others get to heaven. Because light exposes dark (v. 13), Paul teaches that our lives should be a beacon of light that awakens others who are trapped in darkness (v. 14). Sin will be exposed by Christ's example in us, giving others an open door to meet Jesus. Paul adds, "Look carefully then how you walk, making the best use of time because the days are evil" (v. 15, 16).

Light Your World by Being Pure

Isn't this a thrilling opportunity? Have you ever been to a candle lighting service, maybe for Christmas Eve or another occasion? One candle is lit at the front of the room, and the person holding that candle reaches over to his or her neighbor and lights that person's candle ablaze. Then that person lights the candle in the hand of someone else, and so on until the entire room is full of light and every candle is lit. We can be the first candles in the room. We can let our flame ignite others. Christ can really change the world through our dedication to sexual purity.

Of course, you and I know it isn't easy. What should our lives look like if we make the decision to follow Jesus and be pure to His Word, especially in this day when sex is everywhere you turn? First, we must acknowledge that we don't have room for ambiguity and compromise. Often, when we are unsure about whether something is sexually inappropriate, we like to label it as something in the "grey area." But Paul says it is either light or darkness. If you allow your thoughts, associations, and actions to lead you into sin, you are part of that darkness.

But be of good cheer. As long as we allow Jesus to work in us, He will not stop making us shine brighter every day by overcoming challenges. Amidst all the temptations, we need to be "confident of this very thing, that he which hath begun a good work in you will perform it until the day of Jesus Christ" (Philippians 1:6). We will be tempted, and we may feel weak or inadequate. But for this reason, the Lord grants us His Spirit to overcome. That's why Paul exhorts us to be "filled with the Spirit" (Ephesians 5:18).

We can win every battle when we are filled with the Holy Spirit. Think that is impossible? Do you have a track record that indicates otherwise? I hope you'll remember the ones who doubted the shepherd boy who became a king who said,. "Who is this uncircumcised Philistine that He should defy the armies of the living God?" (1 Samuel 17:26). David overcame Goliath. Even if the temptation to sin feels like a giant, the Lord will win through us if we let Him.

Finally, remember that your desire to be pure must come from a love for God and the gift of His Son in your life. "So believers, light of the world, address each other with psalms and spiritual songs, singing and making melody to the Lord with all your heart, giving thanks always and for everything to God the Father in the name of our Lord Jesus Christ, submitting to one another out of reverence for Christ" (Ephesians 5: 19-21). Paul ends with love and the submitting spirit of Christ (vs. 1-2, 21).

So rejoice—you are the light of the world. Christ lives in you so that you might reject all the influences of sexual darkness. Do you want to be the light of the world? Make that decision right now. Choose a life of sexual purity. You are the light of the world.

CHAPTER THREE

The Good News About Love

Since therefore Christ suffered in the flesh, arm your-selves with the same way of thinking, for whoever has suffered in the flesh has ceased from sin so as to live for the rest of the time in the flesh no longer for human passions, but for the will of God. —1 Peter 4:1, 2

In the previous chapter, we briefly looked at the idea of coveting someone sexually as being a form of idolatry. When lustful desires are stirred by appearance, those who foster and dwell upon that lust are making an object out of another person. When sexual objectification happens, a dangerous transformation takes place in the mind. No longer is the person of interest viewed as a child of God, but rather a thing admired for sexual beauty alone.

That's why I want to talk about true love versus infatuation. Lots of people are convinced they can tell the difference, but it isn't that easy sometimes. It happens that when hormones are raging, lust and infatuation can seem a lot like love. And of course, Hollywood does a great disservice by equating lust with true love. The problem is that many people think they are in love when really they are merely infatuated. Sadly, these people will make life-altering decisions based on something that isn't love.

So right now, let's compare Hollywood lust to what the Bible says about true love. And you'll find no better definition of love than 1 Corinthians 13. "Love is patient and kind, love does not envy or boast; it is not arrogant or rude. It does not rejoice at wrongdoing, but rejoices with the truth. Love bears all things, believes all things, hopes all things, endures all things. Love never ends" (vs. 4–8).

Even with a quick reading of this passage, we can glean that love isn't easy—it's developed by service and submission. Every characteristic is one that must develop over time. Without time, we wouldn't have to bear all things, be patient, hope, or endure all things. Infatuation is instant attraction that flames out, but love is the slow rise of respect and eternal attraction. Thus love, not infatuation, should be the basis for marriage and sex.

The Bible might say it this way about infatuation: "It is instant gratification. Infatuation is quick to decision, is blind, does not wait, does not evaluate. Infatuation is intense, irrational sexual attraction. Infatuation is waiting by the phone for hours to make sure you don't miss your beloved's call. Infatuation is butterflies in your belly, and sweaty palms. Infatuation is that 'lighter than air' feeling, and the overwhelming sense of dreaminess, and romance. Infatuation does not give time to decide; it lives in the moment. Infatuation is selfish and jealous. Infatuation makes another person the object of your worship. Infatuation fails."

God Ordained

True love isn't something felt with just the body. Love is a holy principle that is different than feelings of attraction and impulse. Love does not die suddenly when challenged by difficult circumstances, but lust surely does. When the storms of life blow against the foundations of love, it neither waivers nor moves. But infatuation does.

One author writes,

"True love is not a strong, fiery, impetuous passion. On the contrary, it is calm and deep in its nature. It looks beyond mere externals and is attracted by qualities alone. It is wise and discriminating, and its devotion is real and abiding. Love is a precious gift, which we receive from Jesus. Pure and holy affection is not a feeling, but a principle. Those who are actuated by true love are neither unreasonable nor blind.

"Mildness, gentleness, forbearance, long-suffering, being not easily provoked, bearing all things, hoping all things, enduring all things—these are the fruit growing upon the precious tree of love, which is of heavenly growth. This tree, if nourished, will prove to be an evergreen. Its branches will not decay, its leaves will not wither. It is immortal, eternal watered continually by the dews of heaven" (E.G. White, *Letters To Young Lovers*, p. 30).

A wise man once said, "Love at first site is often cured by a second look." The Bible concurs, "The heart is deceitful above all things, and is desperately sick; who can understand it?" (Jeremiah 17:9). When we meet someone new, it feels really good. We get butterflies in our stomach. It is as exciting as anything there is—better than music, better than the movies. But it cannot really be love. It's blunt, but there is no such thing as love at first site. That's the problem: Having pre-marital sex isn't based on love, but infatuation, and sex should be about love.

One young man asked me, "Why shouldn't we have sex? We are going to be together forever. Doesn't God honor that commitment?" But when I asked him how long he had been with the girl, he admitted that it had been less than a few months. I'm here to tell you, that's not long enough. And sure enough, after the infatuation had worn off, this couple found out that they were not compatible. They realized they had been blinded by infatuation. They were so deluded that even an angel standing in from of them couldn't have convinced them otherwise. Yet a little while later, they broke up! Can you imagine the heartbreak they incurred by introducing sex into the relationship?

Heart Matters

As Jeremiah 17:9 teaches, our hearts cannot be trusted. It is desperately sick, and it will make the rest of you sick if you lean on it too much in your decision making. Instead, we have to trust something solid to get us through life and sex unscathed. The Bible says that we need to love; the world tells us we need to lust. But relationships based on lust don't last. Infatuation cannot carry you through the storms of life. It will flee as soon as it can.

Adults and youth have the same problem. Infatuation is such a great feeling, we'll spend time, money, and resources to secure that other person in our lives. It's an adrenaline rush of passion and romance. No one is immune to the idea that we will spend the rest of our lives with a person based on a first date. Look at all the breakups with 20- and 30-something

Hollywood stars. They divorce and break up every other week. Don't be like them. Guard your heart against infatuation, and guard your body against the temptations of lust.

Trust that God's plan will work out best in your life. He is the only solution for our foolish hearts. Otherwise, you may get caught up in something and discard other important areas of your life, even God and your family, putting all your time and energy into a person and based on what could be just a passing feeling. Can you imagine regretting for a lifetime something you did based on infatuation?

Acting on Infatuation

So many people, young and old, make decisions that will destroy their lives and goals based on a mere good feeling. Let's do our best to avoid that by giving our hearts over to someone who we are told will always love us.

Jesus cares deeply about your life and relationships. He is willing to lead you, even when your relationship is new. Let Him be the guiding force. Don't ever feel that anything is too simple or too stupid to involve God in. He cares about every beat of your heart, and He certainly cares about your relationships and your sexual purity.

Of course, with this comes the responsibility to do what God says and to hear His counsel. Many times when we ask God for guidance, He gives an answer we don't like. We try to out think God, getting ourselves to believe that what we think is best "must be" in God's will. Yet we must be open to God, even if it hurts. So what are some ways to draw closer to God and help you avoid making a mistake you'll regret?

1. **Pray.** Prayers must be lifted up to God at every stage in every relationship, including the beginning when hormones are likely at their strongest. Ask Him to

give you patience to determine if all the components of love are really there in your relationship before getting trapped into the sin of pre-marital sex.

2. **Listen to friends and family.** If they have opinions on your relationship, welcome them. You may not always agree, but give an open ear. This may be God's way of giving you guidance, especially if more than two people are saying the same thing.

3. **Spend time in groups.** Allow a real friendship to develop between yourself and the person you are interested in. New couples often run off to spend countless hours alone, like having a private picnic by the lake. But that's dangerous when you're dealing with infatuation. So spend time in groups, around your parents, friends, and family. Not only will you get to know that person better, but those who know you will be able to have better insight. Spend a limited amount of time alone together, and when alone, make sure it's at a restaurant, mall, or church. This will limit opportunity for moments of weakness and temptation.

4. **Don't spend every free moment together.** This one may be hard, but use your God-given will power to make it happen. Being away from each other will give you time to reflect. And the time you do spend together will mean more and will be better spent. Besides, if you have all of your dates and adventures before marriage, you'll have less to do after you're married.

5. **Give it time and talk.** It really takes time to understand someone, to get to know them on a deeper level.

Talk about future plans, thoughts, dreams, and values. You'll be glad you did. Can you imagine becoming intimately involved with someone who you realize you don't really like? Be sure you share a common faith and values. What are your feelings about children? All this stuff must be discussed when considering a mate. This will help you decide if the person is someone you just like to spend time with or is this someone you really can trust and rely on for the rest of your life.

6. Set boundaries. Let each other know ahead of time where you stand on physical contact, how much time you will spend together, what your expectations are, and that the center of your relationship is God. A conversation on this topic can be a bit uncomfortable, but think of the alternative. You might not be able to stop physical contact in the middle of it. It is so much easier to stop it before it starts.

A sprinter running the 100-yard dash flies down the track. If 95 yards into the race, someone shouts, "Stop!" will that sprinter be able to stop on a dime, or will his momentum carry him the 100 yards? Like a sprinter, sexual activity in relationships tends to build momentum. People have a hard time stopping after that momentum has begun.

Be True
The only relationship that will ever last is one based on love. If you really want to see love, visit a couple who has been married for 40, 50, or 60 years. That is true love. They are satisfied just by being in each other's company. They don't love because of appearance, but because of the other person's heart. If you want true romance, that's it. Indeed,

sexual activity is not often a part of the relationship, yet they could not imagine life without their loved one. That is a deep, trusting respect. This is the opposite of infatuation. Love never fails.

That's the kind of love that God has for you. "He heals the broken hearted, and binds up their wounds" (Psalm 147:3). The God of the universe is concerned about you, your life, and your future. He knows when you are anxious and when your heart aches. Even when it hurts to let go of an infatuation, God will be there to comfort you. Even when it hurts to do His will, He will reward you for not forsaking Him.

Please make Him a part of your decisions, especially when they involve love and sex. He's knows all about love—the kind of love that lasts forever. He is the cosmic romancer of all our souls. His love runs so deep that no matter what happens in your life, His love for you remains firm. "For all have sinned and fall short of the Glory of God" (Romans 3:23). Yet, God is Love (1 John 4:8) and He still loves us. That's not infatuation, so let's do our best to mirror that in our relationships.

Remember to pray, read your Bible, and keep your family and God involved when you are beginning a relationship. Many relationships begin with infatuation. That's okay; how else could we get interested in each other? But we can't make an idol of one another, objectifying and sexualizing each other. There is a better way. If you make Jesus the only object of your worship, then turning a relationship into long-lasting love will be possible. And sex is most fulfilling with someone you truly love. It always will be, so make decisions based on God's direction, not on fleeting infatuation.

CHAPTER FOUR

@

The Good News About STDs

For you are bought with a price. So glorify God in your body. —1 Corinthians 6:20

Is a frank discussion about sexually transmitted diseases (STDs) in a book about sexual purity and abstinence really necessary? Is it just a scare tactic to keep kids from having fun? And does it hold any basis for making a heartfelt dedication to God for a life of sexual purity?

Obviously, I think STDs are a crucial topic when talking about sex from a Christian perspective. That's why it's in the book. And it sure might be scary, but it isn't meant to terrify you into obeying the Lord. That decision should come from your heart. But in a culture that wants you to always act on impulse, many young people will take extreme risks like premarital sex without considering the consequences. "It won't happen to me," they think.

However, an STD epidemic is sweeping the world. Parents, young people, teachers, and pastors are not well informed about the issue, and it's time for that to change. Our bodies are not our own; instead, they belong to God (1 Corinthians 2:18, 19). We often get this verse in a talk about diet, alcohol, drugs, and exercise, but rarely do we hear it presented in the context of sexual activity and the health consequences of sinful sex. But we will be held equally accountable, in this life and the next, if we aren't careful in our Christian attitude toward sex.

The STD Crisis

In the United States today, 65 million people are infected with an incurable STD. There are 15 million new cases of STDs every year (CDC, 2000), and one quarter of those are among teenagers. Indeed, young people (ages 15–19) have the highest rate of sexually transmitted diseases of any age group (CDC, 2005). About one out of every four Americans has a sexually transmitted disease.

Scientists claim they cannot pinpoint the direct cause of the pandemic, but it really is simple. Paul teaches that God will let people chase their lusts (Romans 1:28); in other words, He will let us suffer the consequences of our sin-filled decisions. And STDs are often a consequence for living a sexual lifestyle outside of God's plan. God does not want you to suffer, but you have freewill, and one bad decision can affect you the rest of your life in so many painful ways.

What's worse, did you know that many people infected with an STD have no visible symptoms? It's true! Many people have an STD and don't even know it, meaning a person you have sex with can pass an infection along to you without even knowing they have it (CDC, 2005). Moreover, the younger a person is when they first have sex, the more partners they will likely have over their lifespan, increasing the risk of getting and spreading an infection. And what you think might be making you safe from STDs, really isn't. We'll talk more about that later.

Suffering the Consequences

Let's take a moment to present some common STDs and their prevalence. In the very least, it will give you the tools to make a fair risk assessment of what it might mean to have sex with someone before you're married. And keep in mind that many of the sexually transmitted diseases discussed herein can be transmitted through any sexual act, not just intercourse.

1. **Chlamydia.** At least two million people, men and women, are infected with this bacterial STD. Three million more will contract it in the next year (CDC, 2005). If gone untreated, Chlamydia can result in Pelvic Inflammatory Disease and can cause infertility and even death. The only way to ensure not getting Chlamydia is to not have sexual activity.

2. **Gonorrhea.** About 650,000 people become infected with this bacterial infection each year. Like Chlamydia, Gonorrhea can result in Pelvic Inflammatory Disease. It can also cause other major problems for pregnant women, even causing spontaneous abortions. The rates of Gonorrhea have risen dramatically in recent years, especially in the teenage population (Kaiser Family Foundation, 1998). The only way to avoid unwanted disease before marriage is to abstain from sexual activity until marriage.

3. **Genital Herpes.** An incurable viral infection, genital herpes can cause painful outbreaks of lesions or sores. About 45 million people have genital herpes in the nation (CDC, 2005). Many do not know they have it because symptoms do not always appear or are delayed in appearance. Those who are infected can transmit the virus to others without knowing it. It can also be spread through skin-to-skin contact. The wild spread of this particular disease is a testament to the reckless sexual attitudes and behaviors prevalent today. One can only avoid infection by following God's plan of waiting for sexual activity until marriage.

4. **Human Papillomavirus.** Five to six million people have this viral infection. It is said to be the major cause of Cervical Cancer I, which kills 4,000 women every year (National Cancer Institute, 2006). In other words, most of the 4,000 women who will die could have avoided this STD and cancer had they and their husband saved sex for marriage.

But Wait, There's More!

These diseases are only the tip of the iceberg. Hepatitis, Syphilis, HIV/AIDS, and Trichomonas are other common STDs feasting on the young and old—specifically, those who do not adhere to the biblical plan of sexual purity.

Don't think any of these could happen to you? Well, ask the 65 million people in the United States who once thought the same thing. In fact, while you're at it, you can also ask them about one of the biggest lies that Satan likes to sell to young people—"safe sex" propaganda.

Whether it is in the form of condoms or the pill, we're being given a lot of misleading information. Did you know not one form of over-the-counter or prescribed birth control provides 100-percent protection against disease and pregnancy? (The only thing that offers that is abstinence!) In fact, the pill offers no protection from STDs.

Considering the following disclaimer on the package of a popular brand of condoms: "Although no prophylactic or contraceptive can guarantee 100% effectiveness … when properly used, [brand of condom] *may* prevent the transmission of diseases and pregnancy" (emphasis supplied). You can throw me in the middle of the Atlantic Ocean with a life vest, and I *may* survive.

Those who present birth control as protection have a different definition of protection than the one most of us use. You see to them, "protection" really means "risk reduction," and it certainly doesn't mean safety. Are you ready to submit your future health to "risk reduction" for STDs and pregnancy?

Let's take a quick look at some facts provided by the National Institute of Health. This governmental agency conducted a forum to survey condom effectiveness. These were just some of their eye-opening conclusions:

- "Always" users of latex condoms significantly *reduced the risk* of HIV in men and women by 85 to 87 percent.

- Consistent condom use *could* reduce the risk of gonorrhea in *men*. (These studies showed no risk reduction for women!)

- There is no evidence that condom use reduced the risk of HPV infection.

- For other diseases: There is "insufficient evidence from the epidemiological studies on these diseases (Gonorrhea in women, Chlamydia infection, and Trichomoniasis) to draw definite conclusions about the effectiveness of the latex male condom in reducing the transmission of these diseases."

- Only abstinence provides 100-percent safety.

(NIH, July 2001)

I could go on, but you get the point. Don't go against the Word of God because a few humans think they can get away with sinning without suffering the consequences. With or without a condom or the pill, you're playing Russian roulette by having sex before marriage. Except, the odds are much worse than that. With Russian roulette, you have a 1-in-6 chance of harm; with sexual activity before marriage, you have a 1-in-4 chance.

Fool Proof

There is no man-made way to provide complete safety with a risky lifestyle. And sexual activity before marriage is a risky lifestyle. The only way to ensure you don't get addicted to heroin is to not use heroin. Sexual activity before marriage is like heroin. The only way to avoid the health problems associated with alcohol is to avoid alcohol. If God wants you to be healthy, does He want you to be doing something that could lead to infertility, infection, and death?

Most important, can you be a light to the world while living a life full of sinful risks? No, you can't. But more than that, you are not really risking your own body, but Christ's. Jesus bought us with His blood (1 Corinthians 2:18, 19). If you love Him, why put the body that He purchased at risk for diseases that can be avoided by waiting to have sex until marriage, the plan He instituted at creation?

Jesus is calling you and me to a life more abundant (John 10:10), not a life full of disease, heartache, and worry. All worry of sexual diseases and unwed pregnancy can only be erased by choosing a life of sexual purity. He wants what is best for you (John 10:10). And there is no chance of acquiring unwanted sexual disease if you would just stick to His plan for sexual activity. So let us obey His plan out of love and dedication, for we are the light of the world (Ephesians 5:8).

CHAPTER FIVE

The Good News About Sexual Bonding

Sex, scientifically speaking, is a "bonding" experience. During sex, the chemical oxytocin is released in the brain. There are only two other activities that cause this potent of a release of this chemical: child labor and breast feeding.

Sex, child labor, and breast feeding are God-given, endearing, and intimate activities. If a relationship between two people is broken after one of these activities has taken place, connections in the brain are interrupted and harmed, which causes very real and very serious changes. It takes years to reconnect and heal this damage (Keroack, 2005).

It's not just an idea found in a fairy-tale romance: God made sex so that a person must give themselves completely over to the other person: heart, mind, body, and emotion. When you have sex, you are opening yourself to vulnerabilities that you can't easily reel in again.

Do you want proof? The following account is from a woman who grew up knowing Jesus but didn't dedicate herself to sexual purity. Absent that conviction, she compromised the clear teachings of Scripture based on what she thought was true love. As a result, she felt a tremendous amount of heartache and more. I hope her story will speak to you very clearly about the dangers of premarital sex.

Her Story, Her Words

I was just like any other teenage girl. I spent much of my free time hanging out with friends and talking about boys. We spent hours talking about which boys in school were the cutest, who liked whom, and who was in love. Of course, I really had no need for a relationship nor did I know what having one truly meant. But everyone else seemed to want one, so I guess I decided that I needed one too.

My social life changed a lot after my freshman year. I started hanging out with my older sister and her friends. Her boyfriend was from out of town and was attending the local junior college. He would often bring his friends to our house. I grew very close to these guys—much like adopted brothers.

However, that all changed when one evening, one of the boys, Steve, put his arm around my shoulder as we were watching a movie. I talked with my mom about it, and she decided to call him to ask about his intentions. I was mortified!

But after discussing things with Steve and my dad, my parents decided it was okay to see where this friendship might go under their supervision. My parents had gotten to know Steve well the past two years and respected him. He came from a large, churchgoing family and was working his way through college. He was smart, diligent, caring, and very charming. We began writing letters to each other and soon enough, we were "officially" together.

Going into the relationship, I knew Steve was sexually experienced. It made me nervous because I wasn't ready for the things he had already done. We discussed it, and he made it clear that he would never pressure me into anything.

Getting Physical

We saw each other every other weekend or so, and it wasn't long after that we had our first kiss. Since my parents trusted him, we would go out to dinner or to the movies alone in his car.

Well, just a little more than a year into our relationship, I lost my virginity to him. Like a lot of young people say, "It just happened." I was raised in a devout Christian home. I had faith in God and prayed regularly. I tried to live a life according to His will, following the commandments and repenting when I sinned.

Prior to each time Steve and I got physical, I had to justify the act in my head. "We are in love," and "we are going to get married anyway." I remember the first time I tried to confess my sin after I had sex with him. I was very embarrassed to confess it, so I never did. That should have been a big warning.

Dire Consequences

I was living in deep denial, and it caused a ton of mental and spiritual stress. No young person should have to go through that. It seems crazy now, but after the first time, I felt obligated to have sex with Steve in the future. It seemed too late to take it back even though I wanted to. Little did I know, this experience established a pattern of behavior for my future relationships.

When I was 17, a year after I first had intercourse, I went to a gynecologist. One of the tests they performed came back with questionable cells. After another test, they decided to do a very unpleasant biopsy and a procedure to rid my cervix of abnormal cells they said could lead to cancer. The doctor explained that the procedure would cause some scar tissue, but he did not think this would impact my ability to have children. Still, I was shocked! I didn't know sex could ever damage my ability to have children. It was a very scary experience.

After many more trips, my mom privately asked the doctor what was causing these problems. After one appointment, my mom confronted me in the parking lot. My problems were being caused by an STD called HPV. I immediately felt terrified, like I was damaged goods. I didn't sleep around like some other girls I knew, and Steve said he was tested and "clean."

I didn't think my day could get any worse, but it did because I had to tell Steve. My family was on vacation at the time when he came to see me. I remember sitting down in one of the bedrooms and feeling absolutely devastated and embarrassed. It isn't the kind of problem a young lady should be worrying about.

Broken Relationships

Steve and I eventually got engaged. I was only 19 at the time, so we were going to wait to have the wedding until after I graduated from college. But during the fall of my senior year, I called off the wedding. I decided I was too young to be tied down.

One of my justifications for having sex with Steve was that we were going to be together forever. We weren't. I felt guilty and ashamed that I had such intimate relations with him and that things did not work out.

I had many other forms of emotional pain as well: regret, guilt, anxiety, heartache, depression, loneliness, and on and on. I felt physical pain too; I felt sick to my stomach, tired, shaky, and sad. This lasted a very long time; it interrupted my life as I knew it. I had formed my life around a boy. What would I do now without him?

I had no idea how much it would hurt to end a relationship that I was supposed to have for the rest of my life. I had sealed that commitment with my body, and now that commitment was broken, and my body felt the same way. I went through the next few years of my life continuing to make the same mistake too. What a risk I took for the pleasure of a moment.

The Story Isn't Over

It's kind of sad, but obviously true: People don't marry their high school sweethearts anymore. In the past, when you got together in high school, it was likely you were going to get married to that person. But needs have changed, and because young men and women must go to college, and other factors, patience is more important than ever when choosing to have sex.

Like this young lady, when people are in a relationship, they never think it will end. But if we are ever really honest with ourselves, we only actually know we are going to marry someone when we are standing at the altar making our vows.

So when you say, "We are going to get married some day anyway, so we can have sex," it does not make any sense, because you *don't* know!" That's the same mistake our case study made. And it's one you should avoid.

Special Note: There is more to her story that you need to know, and you'll have a chance to read the rest of it in chapter seven. Whatever you do, and no matter where you are in life, don't skip that chapter!

CHAPTER SIX

The Good News
About the Lies

For we do not wrestle against flesh and blood, but against principalities, but against the rulers, against the authorities, against the cosmic powers over this present darkness of this world, against spiritual forces of evil in heavenly places. —Ephesians 6:12

A suave thief runs from his adversary, sprinting up the steps of a tall building. At last he makes it to the top and steps out onto the roof. Frantic, he runs to the ledge and carefully peers over the edge. He's running out of time. He looks around to see his adversary hot on his tail … a dozen stories high, he realizes he has no choice. He makes the leap!

As he free falls, his decent is suddenly broken by an awning, and then another, and then another—tearing through cloth as his rate of decent slows dramatically. Finally, with some good luck, he drops into a truck hauling away cardboard.

He smiles and waves at his duped enemy, and then the screen fades to black.

I'm sure you agree that is a silly situation. But we see it every day, in some iteration in the media. In this case, we're being sold invincibility in a television commercial—we can live a life full of risks and not worry about the consequences. We can be glib toward those things that can hurt us most and be just fine.

But funny or not, if we're tuned into popular culture through television, radio, or video games, we are being influencing in how we think and in what we do. The influence is obvious—it's in our clothing, our language, our behavior—all largely patterned by what is trendy.

No Such Thing as Casual Sex

Here's another pop-culture scenario that's a little more realistic. A single, unattached guy wakes up after a heavy night of drinking and partying. But something is amiss this morning; he looks around to find that there is a strange girl in bed with him! "Who are you?" he asks in a fright. "Who are you?" she retorts, jumping out of bed and putting on her clothes. She flees without an answer out his door. Relieved, the guy says nonchalantly, "Call me!"

We're supposed to laugh at this, but it isn't funny when you really look at the situation in the real world. What does this scene really say about the people involved?

- **Risk Without the Risk:** How many times in television will this man get a random girl pregnant ... or how many times do characters like him get an STD?

- **Emotional Disconnect:** This man has no feelings for this girl. It does not matter to him who she is. He's probably just hoping she won't accuse him of sexual misconduct.

- **Sex is No Big Deal:** Sex is portrayed as something you can get, not something you cherish. It's an encounter that the man thinks is funny and will get a laugh about later with his friends.

- **The Girl Who Doesn't Matter:** Although Hollywood now celebrates women who sleep around, what does it make of the other person involved in this segment? Her shock and confusion is mocked. What a terrible thing to do to a person!

A study by the University of North Carolina, which I call the "Well, Duh!" study, has linked exposure to sexual content in the media to sexual behavior in the lives of young people (*Journal of Pediatrics*, 2006). The study concluded that white adolescents who view sexual content are more than twice as likely to have sexual intercourse by the time they are 14 years old.

Thus science confirms what the Bible has been saying all along: We are changed by what we behold (2 Corinthians 3:18). But when I ask young people if they are influenced by TV, movies, and music, the usual answer is no. When talking with their parents, they say that as long as they can talk to their child about the sex they see on television, watching it really isn't that big a deal.

Why It Really Matters

But they are wrong, and I know from personal experience. I grew up playing baseball, from little league to college ball, and I never once played on the Sabbath day. The opportunities God gave me to witness were immense—players, coaches, and writers, even at the major league level, were able to hear the message of Jesus Christ as a result of my ability to throw a baseball.

I also loved to watch baseball on the television. In the late 80s, a trend in Major League Baseball began to develop: When certain players hit a homerun, they'd start strutting (instead of running) proudly to first base. Whatever their reasons, to an impressionable young man, it looked like a lot of fun. Forget that it is being a poor sport and is flat-out an example of unchristian arrogance, it looked cool to me!

In my second year of college baseball, I created a name for myself. I felt a career in pro-ball was actually in my future. One day, we were playing one of the top schools in the nation. The opposing pitcher was struggling. As I came up to the plate, the other team's manager went out to the mound to discuss options with his pitcher.

While they were talking, I was thinking about what the pitcher might toss up to me. Being a pitcher myself, I knew that whenever my coach came out to the mound to calm me down, I always threw the next pitch right down the middle. I believed this pitcher would do the same.

When he was ready to go, I dug in to the batter's box. He wound up and threw the ball—and sure enough, the pitch was traveling in the exact path I had predicted. I swung as hard as I could, and I connected on the sweet spot. The ball flew, the crowd cheered, and I knew that it was going a long way!

That's when pop culture took over. I decided to strut a little, just like those guys on television. Instead of running, I soaked up the honor. Why, I had just hit a home run and I had plenty of time to get around the bases. Until, well, it didn't sail over the fence.

To my horror, it hit about a foot down from the top of the center field wall. I should have made it to second or even third base while the ball was in the air, but because I was showing off like those guys on TV, I only made it to first. I was humiliated. I stood on base looking at the ground, not wanting to look up. This was not a good witness to my non-Christian teammates either. I felt awful!

As funny as this true story is, it fits nicely into our theme here. You see, my father often watched ballgames alongside me. He pleaded with me to not act like those baseball pros who behaved so unsportsmanlike when they hit a homerun. He told me to always run to first base, no matter how hard I hit the ball. But when it came my turn to make a personal decision, I chose to do what I had seen. By beholding, I was changed.

God taught me a valuable lesson: I would have to suffer the consequences of my poor decisions in every area of life. When we allow sexually impure thoughts and actions enter our minds via music, TV, movies, and whatever, we become changed whether we have other positive influences or not.

The Wasteland

Why do so many young people find Bible study so boring? Why are churches bringing in stadium lights and drums and dry ice and all the bells and whistles into their worship service? Because by beholding pop culture, we have been changed.

Consider the following:

- The average American watches more than seven hours of TV per day.

- The average child in America will spend more time watching TV by the age of 5 than he or she will talk to their father in an entire lifetime.

- The average American will spend a total of 10 uninterrupted years watching TV over their lifespan (Medved, pg.19).

Isn't that horrible? Well, this is even worse!

- In the top 20 shows among teen viewers, at least eight in ten include some sexual content. Nearly half depict sexual behaviors, with one in five showing sexual intercourse.

- Sexual content in sitcoms shot up from 56 percent in 1999 to 84 percent in 2000.

- Shows aimed at teens are the second highest programs (behind soap operas) in sexual activity frequency. Since most of these shows have a teen as a central character, it's easy for teens to identify with the protagonist.

- Top teen shows average 6.7 scenes per hour with sexual content.

- In 2003, 32 percent of all shows included some kind of sexual content (Kaiser Family Foundation, 2003).

Don't you think that 10 years of impure sexual indoctrination is too much for Christians? And we can't forget about the movies, music, and video games either. For those dedicated to living a Christian lifestyle, this is simply wrong. The

Bible says, "Finally brothers ... whatever is true, whatever is honorable, whatever is just, whatever is pure, whatever is lovely, whatever is commendable, if there is any excellence, if there is anything worthy of praise, think about these things" (Philippians 4:8).

Every day our culture tells us that sex outside marriage is just fine. Acting on lust and instant gratification are the way to go. You can have sex today with one partner and move on to another the next day. Pop culture wants to tell us that there are no real consequences to a risky sexual lifestyle. It points a finger of blame at people who want to promote sexual abstinence and point out the lies of "safe sex." For them, sex is merely an animalistic urge and nothing more.

Be Different

At one point, it was popular culture to believe the world was flat. The Bible didn't teach it, but that's what people believed. You were different and dumb to believe otherwise, but was it the truth?

If not agreeing that sex before marriage is good makes you different, then good for the different people. In fact, feel free to call me weird and different. That's what Christ calls us anyway—we are His peculiar people! Jesus' attitude toward love, sex, and marriage would not be accepted today. Let's be like Jesus, shall we?

We already know that sex before marriage is dangerous. It can lead to disease and unwanted pregnancies. It can ruin your goals. It can break your heart. So why are we so willing to accept it by what we watch. This was one of Paul's warnings—don't associate with impure things. Instead, let us seriously and prayerfully consider what we allow into our minds.

Colossians 3:5–8 says, "Put to death therefore what is earthly in you: sexual immorality, impurity, passion, evil desire, and covetousness, which is idolatry. On account of these the wrath of God is coming. In these you too once walked, when you were living in them. But now you must put them all away: anger, wrath, malice, slander, and obscene talk from your mouth."

If we are to be the light of the world, we can't dim that light with entertainment that fractures our connection to Jesus. Worse, by willingly taking these images into our minds, we're inviting temptation into our lives. How many times have you heard someone say something like this on television: "I really respect your decision to not drink and have sex"? We're made to be fools in the media; do you really believe that Jesus, the God of peace and love, was such a fool? We call ourselves Christians so let's follow in His footsteps.

Trendy media is constantly attacking our will to remain faithful in our Christian walk. How can these things be "put to death" if we are allowing them to live on in our music and on our televisions? Are your defenses being weakened by Satan's lies in the media? By beholding, we are changed. He knows that as well as anyone else! He knows the more we become like him, the less we will be like Jesus. We won't be different; we'll be like most everyone else!

So I want you to consider the messages that are being sent to you through the media you enjoy. Are they holy, just, and good—or are they something else? Do they brighten the light shining from inside you, or are they dimming it so that you light is imperceptible to everyone else?

Pray for guidance. In the recent past, I made my own decision to get rid of movies that were filled with unholy attitudes about sex (even some PG movies). You can do the same; get rid of those things that get in between you and God and get rid of pop culture lies that can hurt you in so many different ways.

The BIG Lie

I feel it is very important to discuss one of the most dangerous and biggest lies hurting young people today. It's a simple lie that ultimately leads to terrible sin and, yes, even disease. It is the belief that only sexual intercourse is sinful, and that sexual touching and oral sex doesn't affect your virginity, purity, or chastity. Nor are they sinful if engaged in before marriage.

This simply isn't true. And I'm about to share with you something that will blow your mind. You see, sexually transmitted diseases are called that because they are sexually transmitted. Now we covered this idea in general a little earlier in another chapter, but the devil, as they say, is in the details:

- Herpes can be spread through skin-to-skin contact, oral sex, and intercourse.

- HPV can be spread through skin-to-skin contact, oral sex, and intercourse.

- Gonorrhea can be spread through all forms of sex, including oral sex.

- Chlamydia can be spread through all forms of sex, including oral sex.

- HIV is spread through all forms of sex, including oral sex.

- Syphilis can be spread through touching, oral sex, and intercourse.

- Hepatitis B can be spread through any sexual activity.

I'm sure you get the point. If a sexually transmitted disease can be spread through activities that some people don't want to admit is sex, who exactly is in denial? Think about having to explain to your spouse someday that even though you have never had sexual intercourse, you still have herpes, HPV, or even HIV.

But there are more than just risks for disease. What about sin itself? Satan wants you to believe that these behaviors aren't sex. Why? Because he wants people to deny the Bible. It's easier to do it a little at a time.

Think I'm wrong? Remember what Paul says about being the light. If you look to the Bible for guidance, you won't be tempted to rationalize your way into something that God does not want you to do for your own good. "Do you not know that the unrighteous will not inherit the kingdom of God? Do not be deceived: neither sexually immoral, nor idolaters, nor adulterers... shall inherit the kingdom of God" (1 Corinthians 6:9, 10). It's a stern but fair warning. And it's time to step away from the lies. Ephesians 5:3 says, "But all sexual immorality and all impurity ... let it not once be named among you."

There is no way around it: God detests sexual sin whether you look it up in the New Testament or the Old. Sexual activity of any kind outside marriage is profane in the eyes of God. (See Leviticus. 21:9, 19:29, Deuteronomy 22:20-29, 23:18, and Exodus 22:16 for some eye-opening texts.) Plus the woman on the beast in Revelation 19 is said to be a "whore," or a sexually impure woman.

Perfectly Pure ... It Is Possible!

Sex inside marriage is holy, pure, and undefiled. Sex is a true gift from God, and it isn't dirty or wrong. He gave husbands and wives sex to enjoy. But that's where it must remain, or we get into so much trouble!

So ask Jesus to help you keep your robe white. Ask Him to keep you from believing the lies of this world. Satan knows that his time is short, and he is doing all he can to spread sexual lies that will lead millions astray. Don't give him the time to convince you by watching profane television, listening to sexually driven music, or visiting sin-filled websites. Turn away from those things, and go do something else constructive.

Make a decision for Christ surround yourself with things that uplift your mind to heaven. "Beloved, if your desire is to give your heart to Jesus, if your desire is to live your life as the light of the world: "Set your mind on things that are above not on things that are on the earth" (Colossians 3:2).

And always remember that abstinence is a personal decision to abstain from *all* sexual activity before marriage, regardless of the past.

CHAPTER SEVEN

The Good News About Starting Over

Create in me a clean heart O God and renew a right spirit within me.   —Psalm 51:10

The amazing thing about being a light in the world is that the light that shines from us also works in us (Acts 26:18). The Holy Spirit empowers Christians to be His beacons of truth, even in a culture that is doing everything it can to make us impure. No wonder Paul says that we are a peculiar people (Titus 2:14). Jesus said the world would not understand His followers, and warned that they would pressure us to bend to their will (Luke 6:22, 23).

But some of us have already been bent. We've failed to remain pure sexually in any number of ways—whether that means sexual activity, impure joking, or lusting in our own minds. Our first response is usually shame, and perhaps it should be. But I want you to remember this: When we accept God's call, He points out those things that are counter intuitive to His light. Whether it is sexual impurity, dishonesty, or whatever, the process is for our own good; He's creating less dark and more light.

I'm no different. I have attitudes and behaviors and thoughts that God exposes when I seek to draw closer to Him. How I ultimately respond to that process will either destroy or enhance my character. We all have struggles. A person's sexual impurity is no different than another person's greed or selfishness, as all are caused by lust (1 John 2:15–17; James 1:15). We should be thrilled that God thinks enough of us to know we can change through His power. If we ever get to the point where we believe God has no more work to do in us, that's when we are in real trouble.

Turning Back the Clock

Let's face facts: Once you lose your virginity, you can never lose it again. But know that even though you cannot be restored physically in that sense, you can be restored spiritually. You and I aren't dealing with all this on earthly terms right now, but on heavenly terms with Christ as Lord and Savior.

King David is a perfect example of someone who did not live up to God's plan for sexual purity. David chose to have sex outside marriage (2 Samuel 11:1–5). He made Bathsheba the object of His desire and gave into His lusts causing myriad of sins. When the prophet Nathan exposed that sin, the king felt the full weight of his impurity. He mourned, "I have sinned against the Lord" (2 Samuel 12:13). As soon as David was able to recognize his sin and was repentant, the prophet Nathan shared this loving message from God: "The Lord has put away your sin."

Likewise, Jesus is in the business of restoring hearts. When you have a renewed heart from God, the only thing that matters is that new heart and what you do with it from there. You might not return to the physical innocence you once had, but there is a deeper, more abiding purity, restoration, and victory in a new life in God. Those who cherish this new heart are promised new bodies when Jesus comes (1 Corinthians 15:50–55). Renewed hearts still cherish and take care of the bodies we have on earth, but they really look forward to the new bodies that will be completely pure, holy, and glorious (2 Corinthians 5:1–10) in the next age to come.

Ephesians 4:24 says, "Put on the new self, created after the likeness of God in true righteousness and holiness." It doesn't matter what has happened in your past. Forgiveness is now, and the old self is gone. All sins can be forgiven from the same source. Jesus wants us to be born again because He wants to free us from all lusts (John 3:3). When we are renewed through repentance and forgiveness, we give ourselves over to His holiness. Where lust brings death, Jesus brings newness of life and a restored relationship with Him.

Remember that no matter the sin, no matter how bad the habit, no matter what, Jesus will forgive and give you a new life. David was called "a man after God's own heart" (1 Samuel 13:14) despite his sin against God and his fellowman.

All you have to do now is ask for forgiveness, and it will be yours (Romans 6). Thank Him by committing to the sexual purity He wants for those who love Him—abstaining from *all* sexual activity until marriage, *regardless of the past*. Run to Him today, because this world cannot provide you purity.

What Grace Really Means

"Blessed are the pure in heart, for they shall see God" (Matthew 5:6). We can't take God's mercy and love for granted. We cannot sin knowing that God will forgive. Indeed, God will forgive a sincere heart, but a person who lets known sin into his or her life, relying on future forgiveness, is digging a big hole.

So the best time to develop your character is now, when you are young. And the only lifestyle that will provide for your greatest success, to achieving all the goals that really matter in your life, is following God's will. Better yet, if you train yourself to follow God's voice in the area of sex, you will set yourself up for success in other areas. The courage, strength, faith, and conviction that you take out of every spiritual and physical battle today is the same courage, strength, faith, and conviction that you will carry with you into every battle of your adult life.

"I have stored up your word in my heart, that I might not sin against you. … I will meditate on your precepts and fix my eyes on your way" (Psalm 119:11, 15). Let us all learn to listen to God's Word, and to make it a part of who we are. If you do that, nothing can stand in the way of your goals.

Revisiting Her Story

Remember the young woman from chapter 5? I wanted to keep the rest of her story until this chapter because it fits the theme of redemption. It's worth reading if you're worried that God can't use you because you have sinned sexually in the past …

I was hired as a youth mentor in my community. I wondered what kind of example I could be to them considering my past. But this was God working in my life to bring me back to Him. He kept nagging me about being a hypocrite, and His Spirit kept getting louder and louder. Even though it had been a few years since I lost my virginity, I decided to regain my purity by making a decision to stick to God's plans for my life.

Not long after, I reconnected with one of my ex-boyfriends who lived out of state. We got back together over the phone, and he decided he was going to move back home so that we could be together. He kept talking as though things would be the same and that we would jump in sexually where we left off. But I kept telling him about my new convictions, and he would say that he understood, but he also would keep bringing it up. I finally told him not to come. I would not go back on my decision to be a "born again virgin," even for him. I was sorry that he did not understand, but I was happy that, for the first time, I really stood up for my convictions.

It was a big temptation from Satan that God helped me to overcome. After I lost my virginity, it was so easy for me to be made to feel guilty about not having sex, so I would sin over and over again. Satan kept accusing me, and I did not know what to do about it until God showed me I could regain my purity. I had won a victory in Jesus. I refused to go back on it.

Not Perfect, But Restored

God blessed me after this by sending my husband. He is a godly man who also made the same sexual mistakes in his past. Together we made a vow to save ourselves this time, and our wedding night was very special because of the decision to wait. It was romantic and amazing.

Of course, one of the most difficult things I had to do was tell my future husband that I had an STD. Patrick understood like a gentleman, but HPV virus still haunts me. Even though I was able to have children and the disease is gone, the scar tissue from the procedures the doctor had to perform made labor even more difficult than it already was.

I will always regret my decision to have sex outside of marriage. I was too young to deal with all the emotions and responsibilities that go with sex. It changes relationships in major ways. I knew deep down I did not want to marry Steve, but I felt I had to stay with him because of the commitment

I made with sex. We had sex because we would be together forever, right? My heart, body, mind, and spirit could never be the same after. I truly wish I had waited to give all of myself to my husband.

But today, I am happy with the life God has given me. He has renewed me with things that I do not deserve. I now have a beautiful family made in marriage! God has blessed me despite my mistakes, and I know that sex is a wonderful experience and is something meant for a husband and a wife to enjoy, because I am enjoying it with my husband.

Restoration For You Too

Jesus wants to take off your filthy rags of sin and worldliness (Zechariah 3:1–7). He wants to replace them with a new robe that is sparkling white, and He longs to put the crown of righteousness on your head!

When you turn from sin to Jesus and ask for forgiveness, He accepts you with open arms, like a father who is welcoming a wayward son. Allow Him to have that relationship with you today, no matter what mistakes you have made in the past.

CHAPTER EIGHT

The Good News About Sex and Marriage

Therefore shall a man leave his father and his mother and shall hold fast unto his wife: and they shall become one flesh. —Genesis 2:24

God knows you really well. He knew you even before you were conceived (Jeremiah 1:5). That should give you a lot of hope, because along with knowing you, He loves you. And because He loves you, He wants you to have the best in life.

And one of the best things you can have in life is a good marriage. One of the other things God knows is who you are going to marry, and perhaps a little more important, who you should marry. He also knows if you have no interest in relationships and marriage, and He's fine with that. In fact, Paul says it is commendable for you to live you life only dedicated to Christ.

But when two of God's children choose to be man and wife, He surely must smile because marriage is holy. In

Scripture, God treats the sanctity of marriage as very special. He instituted marriage at creation (Genesis 2) and ordained that a man should leave his parents and be one with His wife (Genesis 2:24).

More than that, there is great beauty in marriage. Paul likens marriage to Christ loving His church. He says that husbands and wives should serve each other in the same way Jesus came to die for humanity (Ephesians 5:25). The wedding day is also pictured many times in both parables and prophecy (Matthew 25, Revelation 19). Solomon said to his wife, "Set me as a seal upon your heart, as a seal upon your arm, for love is as strong as death... Many waters cannot quench love, neither can the floods drown it: if a man would give all the substance of his house for love it would be utterly condemned" (Song of Solomon 8:6). God loves weddings and marriages. The first recorded miracle from Jesus came at a wedding (John 2).

But God also defends marriage with His law (Exodus 20). Christ says that no man has the authority to put it asunder (Matthew 19:6). If God seeks to protect the sanctity of marriage, shouldn't we? And if sex is a part of marriage, could we be stealing something from the future by having sex today? There are so many troubles that sex before marriage can create in your relationships, even if the one you marry is the one you have been having sex with! But since God loves and respects marriage, so should we.

Envisioning Marriage

What is your picture of your wedding day? Is it a big or small wedding? Is it outdoors or indoors? What colors will be used? Who will you invite? Who will be your best man or your maid of honor? What pastor would you like to perform the ceremony?

But even more important, what type of person would you like to marry? What qualities will they have? What type of personality should they posses? What things do you believe make for a happy marriage? Are there things about your parents' marriage that you would like to imitate in your own some day? Are there some things you would like to do better or differently?

Despite what many people say about marriage, it is permanent (Matthew 19). That's why it is a good idea to make a good decision about who to marry before the wedding day. This is where our discussion of love versus infatuation becomes so important. Many people make life-changing decisions like sex and marriage based on infatuation, not love. With sex before marriage, we're putting the cart before the horse.

One author puts it this way. She wrote it for women, but the theme applies to men too:

> "Before giving her hand in marriage, every woman should inquire whether he with whom she is about to unite her destiny is worthy. What has been his past record? Is his life pure? Is the love which he expresses of a noble, elevated character, or is it a mere emotional fondness? Has he the traits of character that will make her happy? Can she find true peace and joy in his affection? Will she be allowed to preserve her individuality, or must her judgment and conscience be surrendered to the control of her husband? … Can she honor the Saviour's claims as supreme? Will body and soul, thoughts and purposes, be preserved pure and holy? These questions have a vital bearing upon the well-being of every woman who enters the marriage relation.

"Let the woman who desires a peaceful, happy union, who would escape future misery and sorrow, inquire before she yields her affections, Has my lover a mother? What is the stamp of her character? Does he recognize his obligations to her? Is he mindful of her wishes and happiness? If he does not respect the honor his mother, will he manifest respect and love, kindness and attention, toward his wife? When the novelty of marriage is over, will he love me still? Will he be patient with my mistakes, or will he be critical, overbearing, and dictatorial? True affection will overlook many mistakes; love will not discern them" (E.G. White, *The Adventist Home*, p. 47).

Sex Before Marriage Can Hurt Your Marriage

As we discussed earlier, sex can interrupt this period of evaluation. When sex is thrown into a pre-wed relationship, it can cloud up communication with each other and with God. It can blind us to truths about our partner's character that may be dangerous to our long-term happiness. It's like a pastor writing a sermon while high on drugs. Will God speak to him? The further we walk from God, the harder it is to hear His voice. Should we risk that for a moment or two of pleasure?

Marriage is full of so many wonderful things: worshipping God together; raising a family; experiencing true love; and security and trust. Marriage also comes with a lot of responsibility: supporting the family; the emotional well being of your mate; showing each other love, dealing with faults; spending quality time; and others.

Thus it is vital to know who your love is and what drives them. Is God the core of their life or an after thought? Is sex the most important thing to them? If you are being pressured into sex, what does that say about this person as your future spouse? Indeed, you should feel safe and respected more around your future mate than anyone else you have ever met.

In his book, *The Five Love Languages,* Gary Chapman identifies five different ways people give and receive love. Only one of those has to do with physical touch and sex. If you're making sex the focal point of your life before marriage, what happens after marriage? If you're letting sin into your life before marriage, what happens after marriage?

Sex is the pinnacle of a marriage relationship, not the base. When it is relied on as a foundation, it can handicap other equally important parts of your relationship and destroy what could have been a great friendship. Plus, when the storms of life blow and the winds beat hard on a marriage home, the relationship based on sex will die, and the one based on the broad base of love will carry the day and create even more love.

What About Living Together?

Is living with someone the right answer? Consider this: Couples that live together before marriage have a 50-percent higher chance of getting a divorced after they marry than do people who do not live together before marriage. I imagine there is a connection between this fact and the fact that they are not living their lives according to God's plan.

Besides, if people are going to live together, what is holding them back from marriage? There must be some reason they feel they are not ready for the marriage commitment. If they are not ready to marry, they certainly aren't ready to live together. And they certainly aren't ready to have sex!

Many young people I've met have complained, "It's so long to wait until I get married!" Oddly enough, that's very shortsighted thinking. The average age for marriage is 25, so if you're 16 years old, you will wait on average another nine years to have God-ordained sex. Now granted, that seems like a long time. But when you consider the obstacles that sexual activity before marriage can bring to your life, sex is well worth the wait.

Waiting nine years for sex is much better than suffering 64 years with an incurable STD (given an average lifespan of 80 years). Waiting nine years is much better than having to care for a baby before you're married. Waiting nine years is well worth the wait if a lifetime of sex is meaningful and from love, rather than the heartache that comes from a breakup. It's worth the wait if you pick the right partner, something you can't really do if you are already having sex! Think of living with someone for 55 years whom you're really not fond of because you allowed sexual activity to hinder your decision making!

Sex Is a Gift Best Unwrapped on Your Wedding Night

Ever opened a gift before you were supposed to? You open it and it is fun and enjoyable, but when Christmas or your birthday comes around, you felt rotten. On that special day, you won't have the same joy and excitement.

The wedding day is gift day. Will you open your gift for the first time on that day, or will you open it ahead of time and share it with someone that it may not be meant for? Remember, the only moment you know you will marry someone is when you are standing with them at the altar saying your vows. Will you wait to share the most beautiful expression of that love with your husband or wife, or will you share your gift with someone who may not be the one for you?

Sex is good. It is something to look forward to, so long as it is enjoyed in marriage. When sexual activity happens outside marriage, it becomes like a flooded river that spills over into the other parts of your life. It can completely hinder and disrupt your life. Don't let that happen. Protect your future marriage today by remaining pure for God. Be the light.

Chapter Nine

Straight Talk

Let no one despise you for your youth, but set the believers an example, in speech, in conduct, in love, in faith, in purity.   —1 Timothy 4:12

L isten up: A war is being waged over your soul. Do you understand the implications? It is part of that great controversy between good and evil that you have heard so much about. It's not a joke or trivial; it's real. It is a battle over your mind, over your conduct, over your convictions, and it's being waged everywhere that has anything to do with your life—in government, on television, in newspapers, in music, and in schools.

Are you ready to choose a side?

- **Side #1 says** human sexuality is primarily about physical pleasure. The goal is pleasure without consequence, like contracting a disease or having an unwanted pregnancy. Sexual activity is part of growing up and maturing. Submission should be made to these urges as long as some kind of protection is used.

- **Side #2 says** human sexuality is primarily emotional and psychological, not physical. It properly involves long-term emotional bonding, intimacy, and commitment between a man and a woman on biblical grounds.

On what side will you stand? You know, we chose a side even if we don't make an active choice. We can passively take sides by the entertainment we choose, the conversations we are involved in, the jokes we laugh at, and the way we dress. This battle goes deep and it is fought everywhere.

I've Been There With You

Not everyone is "doing it." The Kaiser Family Foundation reports that in 2003 (US Teen Sexuality Report), 66 percent of high school students were not having sex. That means most kids are not doing it. And you also don't need to be in a relationship. You are no less of a person if you don't have a boyfriend or girlfriend. You don't need someone to complete you. In fact, the wise thing is to achieve your non-relationship goals *before* you decide to think about a relationship. Having a significant other can be a real distraction and can pull your time, resources, and thoughts away from your other goals.

When I talk about sex and being pure, I get a lot of young people asking me what I really know about it. Well, I know a lot. As mentioned earlier, I played baseball in college. I had a 90-mile-an-hour fastball, and my goal was playing professional baseball. Reaching that kind of goal takes training, exercise, and mental toughness. Plus if your desire is to remain a Christian in the world of sports, like mine was, it takes a lot of prayer and Bible study.

Like everyone else, I had to overcome some obstacles. But the biggest one was having a girlfriend. Now I am not blaming her or accusing her of anything wrong. We had times of joy and fun, but I allowed myself to be too consumed by the relationship. I gave time to her that I should have given to the training and studying that I needed to do. God had given me all the tools, and I had a choice to make. Would I pursue my goal, or would I pay more attention to distractions?

Like so many young people, I thought I would be with this girl forever. I wasn't. So, look back with me at all of that time, money, and opportunity I spent on a relationship that I was fighting to make work ... but wasn't meant to be. I blew my chance for my dream for a relationship that wasn't going to last! What I failed to realize then was that if it was in God's plan for us to be together, I could have spent much more time pursuing my dream and she would still be there.

The point is that relationships in the life of young people can be limiting. Relationships take away time and effort from things that might be more important. If you are a person that has a goal, it might be best for you to focus all of your attention on that rather than on a relationship. If it's the Lord's will that you be married in the future, don't worry. He will make it happen. Obviously, all your goals should be infused with God in prayer and study. Don't throw away your relationship with God over any earthly goal either.

You don't have to be in a relationship. Be content where you are and pursue those gifts God has given you.

Respect God by Respecting Your Parents

"Children obey your parents in the Lord: for this is right. 'Honor they father and thy mother' ... that it may go well with you, and that you may live long in the land" (Ephesians 6:1–3). It's not popular and it's outdated for the world we live in, but I hope you will respect your parents' input and wishes. The world is pressuring you to have sex before marriage, and it is pressuring you to disrespect your parents. Don't do either, because God has a plan in both that will work if you let it.

Of course, when our parents have an opinion about a friend or relationship, we hate to admit they are right. We hate to hear their advice, but for the most part, they have our best interests in mind. They probably want to see you succeed.

Parents can have a different perspective on friendships and relationships that you can't see. They probably know you better than anyone else you will ever meet. They have the ability to evaluate you, your friends, and your relationships, so listen to what they have to say. Pray that God will help you evaluate their opinions clearly and correctly. It is okay not to agree with every opinion your parents have, but respect them anyway and follow their advice. Grandparents are also a good source of knowledge, so use them too. If your parents have been cruel to you and you don't trust them, find the advice of someone older than you who you can trust and who has a biblical perspective of this world.

Demand that your new acquaintances meet your parents or guardian. Spend time around them with your new friends too. If your closest family and friends have an opinion about a new relationship, listen carefully. They love you, as much as you love them. Don't chance risky friendships ever, but especially with someone who your friends and parents don't like.

GVSL

"Christ's example shows us that our only hope of victory is in continual resistance of Satan's attacks." That might sound like an empty challenge until you read the rest of this amazing passage:

"He who triumphed over the adversary of souls in the conflict with temptation understands Satan's power over the race, and has conquered in our behalf. As an overcomer, He has given us the advantage of His victory, that in our efforts to resist the temptations of Satan we may unite our weakness to His strength, our worthlessness to His merits. And sustained by His enduring might, under strong temptation, we may resist in His all-powerful name and overcome as He overcame" (E.G. White, *Conflict and Courage*, pg. 251).

How could God ask such a thing of us—to resist temptation constantly? The beauty is that Jesus knows our temptations, because He was faced with them too. Hebrews 4:15 reports, "For we do not have a high priest who is unable to sympathize with our weaknesses; but who was in every respect tempted as we are, yet without sin." Jesus wants to give you victory over sexual temptation, because he faced the "lust of the flesh" himself (1 John 2:16). He knows how to win that battle, and He promises you that same victory.

But you must also make a decided effort to do what you can to resist temptation. You must have a strategy to avoid risky situations. Chapter 4 included some effective strategies, and you should keep them close to your heart. But here are some others you can put into your arsenal, something I have called *GVSL*:

G is for God, who must be the first step in all that you do. Ask Him to help you overcome a temptation and to refuse unwanted sexual contact. Pray that God would give you the strength and the words to be victorious. This prayer can be uttered at any time—well before the battle and in the heat of it.

V is for your voice, which sounds the desire to shut off inappropriate TV shows, movies, and music if you are present. Tell someone firmly that you are not interested in sexual contact, situations, or talk. Tell them you don't want to be pressured. If you never say anything, how will they know where you stand?

S is for standing up. Literally get up to leave if you are uncomfortable or cannot find the words to use. If someone persists with pressure, stand up to leave the area. Go find someone else who respects you to be with.

L is for leaving. If pressure or temptation persists, remove yourself from the situation entirely. If you find yourself in a risky situation, like being home alone with someone to whom you are attracted, don't hang around to give the devil time to tempt you. Do not allow yourself to be bombarded with pressure. This can be the very first step if you need it to be.

It's Never Too Late to Do the Right Thing

We live in a world full of pressure to do wrong. Impure sexual activity is on our doorstep in so many forms that I know you might have already lost a battle. But the war is Christ's. Do you understand that?

In John 8, cruel men threw a sinful woman at the feet of Jesus. She had been caught in adulterous sex. She lost the battle, expecting a death sentence. But instead, Jesus won the war for her and offered her peace and restoration: "Neither do I condemn thee; Go and sin no more" (John 8:11). If you desire forgiveness and a life of purity in Jesus, act on it by asking Him today to help you. He's not here to condemn you. He wants you to go forward now and sin no more.

"I am the Light of the world; whoever follows after me will not walk in darkness, but will have the light of life" (John 8:12). Everyone has sinned. Everyone is sinning somewhere in their life, so we are all asked by God to drop what we are doing and follow His Son. That includes turning our back forever on sexual sin.

> "Jesus knows the circumstances of every soul. You may say, I am sinful, very sinful. You may be; but the worse you are, the more you need Jesus. He turns no weeping, contrite one away. He does not tell to any all that He might reveal, but He bids every trembling soul take courage. Freely will He pardon all who come to Him for forgiveness and restoration ...

> "The souls that turn to Him for refuge, Jesus lifts above the accusing and the strife of tongues. No man or evil angel can impeach these souls. Christ unites them to His own divine-human nature. They stand beside the great Sin Bearer, in the light proceeding from the throne of God" (E.G. White, *In Heavenly Places*, pg. 309).

God promises you restoration. Take hold of it right now. Psalm 51:12 says, "Restore to me the joy of your salvation; and uphold me with a willing spirit." He'll not only forgive you, but He'll also hold you up when the battle comes again. His victory includes over former sin, but also future temptation. So don't walk away just because of the guilt of one false move. That's the devil talking. Instead, go to the light, and He will wipe away your guilt. "For everyone who is born of God overcomes the world: and this is the victory that overcomes the world—our faith" (1 John 5:4).

Nice and Easy

Seriously, try not to grow up too fast. Take time to enjoy the blessings God has given you for this time in your life. Take time to grow to know your parents, your family, and your God. Appreciate the innocent beauty, family, and friends He has blessed you with.

Also, don't worry about tomorrow, but plan for it. Take what you need to navigate this world, like this book. Even better, take your Bible and a commitment to pray every single morning and night for the power to say no to the temptations of this world.

Take time to enjoy where you are right now because God has put you here for a specific reason. Figure out what that is. Seek truth and don't let the mixed messages around you confuse you into sexual sin. Don't believe you should have sex because "everyone else is doing it." You are better than that, and God knows it. Be passionate for holy things, and work out your identity with God. Don't be found identifying with the world, because your light will fade and die.

But the Lord's light will shine forever (1 John 1:5–7). So seek God's light, not the world's darkness. The more you look to Christ, the more you will see the difference. Set your mind to sexual purity and victory in Christ.

Stay pure, always. "Thanks be to God, who gives us victory through our Lord Jesus Christ" (1 Corinthians 15:57).

CHAPTER TEN

Straight Talk to Parents

Train up a child in the way that he should go, and when he is old he will not depart from it. —Proverbs 22:6

Having a teenage child is an odd and difficult paradigm. We are seeking to hold on to those precious moments and memories of their childhood, but the reality is that they are seeking and will ultimately gain their independence.

It's a dangerous world out there, and the devil has your child in his sites. One of the most potent temptations for them, boy or girl, is premarital sex. And for the most part, you have to influence them on your own.

Many churches have a wonderful message about healthy eating and exercise, but how often is the message about sexual purity clearly and boldly presented? How often are young people challenged about sexual sin and its consequences? Our church and our families need to rally around God's message of sexual purity

But even if the church with one voice sends a strong message to young people about sexual activity, it's still up to you. That's why this chapter is reserved for you, so that you have the tools you need make sure you bring up your child in the way they should go.

Of course, it isn't easy. Most of us don't even know how to approach the topic, worried that we may become overzealous and make our kids think sex is dirty and bad. Other parents are simple deceived; they think they are doing an adequate job of instructing their kids about sex, but they are not. If you're one of these, this book will help you too. I'm going to give you a little bit of reality and some effective ways to parent your child regarding sexual purity. You need to pay attention, because you child's eternal destiny could very well be at stake.

Kids Will Be Kids

If ever there was a cop out to parenting, "Kids will be kids" is it. I see the phrase as a mechanism that lets parents feel less responsible about what they teach their kids, and it is an attitude that needs to go. Whether it has to do with drugs, alcohol, vandalism, pre-marital sex, or whatever irresponsible behavior, culture likes to say, "kids will be kids."

But it shortchanges our children. It disrespects them. It means that our kids have little or no control over what they do, how they act, or what they say. But God sees it quite differently, calling parents to hold their children to a high standard. "You shall love the Lord your God with all your heart and with all your soul and with all your might. And these words that I command you today shall be on your heart. You shall teach them diligently to your children, and shall talk of them when you sit in your house, and when you lie down and when you rise" (Deuteronomy 6:5–7). He knows your children can love Him if they learn about His law of love; that means your children are smart enough and capable enough to be pure.

To teach your kids diligently leaves no room for "kids will be kids." There is no leverage for you to displace the responsibility. God has entrusted you with the life of your child; He wants you to raise moral people that strive for sexual purity. He wants you to prepare them to walk the narrow road to heaven. It is a gigantic task, but it is the most rewarding experience you will ever know.

Of course, our kids will rebel. It's in their natures; but that doesn't excuse anyone from their sin. We may feel powerless when they beat against our rules, but we are no powerless. Every time you stand your ground and teach them the right thing, the Lord is right there with you, speaking to their hearts. So don't give up, and be sure you give them this message.

Who Are We?

So how do we approach our children with the message of sexual purity? How do we present the message in a loving way that will speak to them where they are? Well, let's breakdown a few facts:

You are the most influential part of your child's life. That's right, you. Not their friends, not their teachers, not anyone else on the face of this earth will mean more than you. The influence you bring to them will guide them through life more than anything. If you are on the fence about something, they too will sit on the fence. It is okay to let your kids know who you are, what your beliefs are, why you believe the way you do. They'll like knowing you better.

Humans have an innate instinct to pick the less restrictive message. If you're given the keys to a sports car, what would you rather hear: "You can only drive the speed limit. If you do, you'll never get hurt or get a ticket"? Or would you rather hear, "Drive it as fast as you want. But you have to wear your seatbelt"? When it comes to sex, we're almost always ready to teach the second option—reducing-the-risk sex … "safe sex." It's natural to choose that because you want your child to like you and think you aren't overbearing. On top of that this is the argument that society tells us is logical.

But this is their eternal destiny at stake. Be a little over-bearing on the important stuff, okay? If you tell your kids that abstinence until marriage is the God-given plan, that it is the healthiest and best choice, you will have made an impression. If you say, "Abstinence until marriage is best, *but if you do get involved sexually*, here are some ways to protect yourself," the influence of abstinence will leave the building. By presenting two messages, most kids will naturally take to the least restrictive. It takes less self-control, so why not? Eve was presented a less restrictive message while she was without sin, yet she made the wrong choice. Your kids have it even harder than Eve. Give them one message.

We are just as uncomfortable as our kids talking about this. It's the stuff of comedies, but it is so much more important than that. You need to talk about it, and you might even need to start today after you finish reading this chapter. The good thing is that the more you do it, the more you build that relationship, the easier it will become. No, it's not a one time talk. You'll have to approached it day after day if that's what it takes to make your kids know where you stand and what you will not accept. Remember that Moses told the people of Israel to talk about God with their kids when they got up, when they laid down, and when they walked by the way.

Don't hesitate to start now. Being uncomfortable will make us hesitate. We can't afford that. If your child is 45 years old and married, it's probably too late. But if you think your child is too young or beyond the age that you can reach them, they generally aren't. Never think that your child is beyond your influence; they are your children, you make a difference.

We cannot share what we do not have. If you are feeble minded when it comes to the topic of sexual purity, get educated. The Lord knows this should not be your only resources when approaching the topic of sex with your kids. Part of being a good educator is knowing your material.

Don't be shy. Finally, I want you to read this over and over until it makes you sick. You probably won't believe it, but stay with me: *Your child wants you to give them a strong message about abstinence.* Our children don't want a "kids will be kids" attitude from you. So stand up for what you believe. Kids don't want you to be just a friend, but to give them a standard they can hold on to. If you respect them and your own responsibility, they will more than likely respect it too.

Practical Guidance

Let's get into some basics. And before we get too far, here's the most important guidance you could ever hear. Without God, we're powerless to help our kids choose the right path when it comes to sexual purity. So you need to pray, and you need to be in the Word. Ask Christ to hide you and give you His words. He knows your child better than anyone, so let Him be your number one resource. If more parents did this, our world would be transformed.

Always keep talk about sexual purity appropriate for the age. It still stands that it is never too early and never too late to start no matter what their age. But you have to keep some rules in mind. For discussion with very young kids, simple talks about health and safety are important. This lets them know that you are concerned with their well-being and is an inroad to establishing some rules for them. They will understand that you really do have their best interest in mind. Along with that, inform your child of some of the changes that they can expect in their body and what they may begin to feel. These simple discussions will set the stage for more in-depth conversations later on.

Begin discussions with simple life questions. Discussing your child's goals, dreams, and ideas is a great way to begin a frank lesson on sexual purity. Share with them lessons you have learned in life. Be real with your kid and let them know that you acknowledge you are not perfect, but that you are closer to Jesus as a result of the lessons you have learned in life.

Never, never, never **justify your mistakes.** This is important. Never say anything that even remotely sounds like pride for the sinful sexual acts of your youth. Always tell your child that if you could do it all over again, you would not have made the same mistakes. Let them know the consequences of your sin and tell them you don't want them to suffer those. If you somehow glorify or even justify the sins of your youth, they may begin to think they have leeway to find out for themselves.

Your mistakes of purity in the past do not disqualify you from setting a standard for your child. Some parents believe that since they have lived less-than-pure lives in the past, they are not qualified or capable of being a mentor. But does a person who burned down his parent's house never tell his kids not to play with matches? Having learned from a bad decision in the past may even make you more credible to your kids. Also, don't let them challenge you on your mistakes in the past. Let them know it's silly to choose sin because someone else did.

Modeling is a major way that children learn habits and skills from parents and other role models. If you have been sexually impure in the past, you have to be different starting right now. Modeling occurs when young people watch parents and role models to pattern their behavior. If you act, believe, and conduct yourself in a specific way, chances are your kids will pick up on that behavior. If you want your kids to remain biblically pure, you must also respect God's plan for sexual purity. If you don't, and your child follows your behavior, you are responsible in the eyes of God.

Talk to your child about an issue before it presents itself in their life. Prepare your child for what is ahead. You may be surprised to find that what you think is ahead in their lives may already be at present. Even if you think an urge, pressure, or issue may be a year or two off, prepare them for it now. Kids are sexualized at a very young age through the media, in school, and in their friendships. Get started now.

Be honest and straightforward. Don't try to answer questions if you don't know the answer. Kids know when you are making up stuff to sound enlightened. They will respect you more for a simple, "I don't know, but I'll find out for you." Also, give them clear, concise answers. If you are asked a question, give the simplest answer you can manage. A liturgical sermon on the issue could put them off. Be real, be straight, and be honest. They'll love you for that, even if they think it is weird.

Respect your spouse. Allow your kids to see that no matter what, your relationship is a rock. Kiss and hug each other in front of your kids. They'll feel love too. You may have disagreements, but support each other's decision. *Do not ever demean each other before your children.* Always show your children that you respect your spouse more than any other person in the world.

Tell your child that God gives them power over temptations and urges. Discuss with them that Jesus loves them and wants them to be healthy and happy. Show them that they exert self-control all the time in other areas of their lives, and they can certainly do it when it comes to sex. When they do a chore, or get to school on time, or do anything that they don't necessarily want to do, they show self-control. Tell them people will respect them more for showing self-control. Tell them that self-control is something to be commended and is never a sign of weakness.

Always point your child to Christ. Never be afraid to point out sin as sin, and point your kids to Jesus for any mistake. Let them know that your forgiveness is free, as is Christ's. If they have made a mistake in the past, let them know how you feel calmly and move on as a family. Let them know that they need to ask Jesus for forgiveness, and also to whomever they may have wronged. Make them feel loved and forgiven, even if what they have done hurts you. To give them this will help them draw closer to you and rely on your advice more, just as they will when we hear about Jesus' forgiveness.

For Dads Especially

If you are a dad, you must exude respect for women in all that you do, say, and think. Make it obvious to your kids that you have a deep, abiding respect for women in your home and outside your home. This will greatly impact the sexual decisions of your sons and daughters.

You also need to let your daughter see that you value her mother greatly. Let her feel that same emotion from you by spending time with her and giving her affection. If you respect and love your daughter, she will choose men who hold those same ideals, men who will honor her purity. She will learn to respect herself and her body and will better know the difference between infatuation and true love.

Empower your daughter with the knowledge that sex is not the only way a man should show love for their wives. Give her the skills to refuse and avoid unwanted sexual contact. If your daughter needs to talk, or if anyone ever hurts her, tell her that she can always come to your loving arms for help.

If you have a son, teach him today that women are not to be dominated, shunned, or disrespected sexually or otherwise. Demand that he respects his sister's and his mother's space, bodies, and thoughts. You can do this by supporting your wife in discipline. Be good to your wife so your boy knows that women aren't just sexual beings and tell him that the only appropriate sexual contact occurs inside marriage.

You have one more crucial responsibility. You are the high priest of your home, the spiritual leader. Do not ever accept sexually driven music, talk, movies, or television programs in your sanctuary. Set a strict standard and tell your children why. If God doesn't want impure things in His temple, you can't have it in yours.

Because you have such a high value in the home, be sure to live what you say. Always show your deep convictions rather than just saying them. Actions speak louder than words. Finally, promote and set a standard for family worship. Always be ready to direct your home to the loving arms of Jesus. Allow your children to see you as both a strict judge and a gracious, loving friend. You are responsible for the spiritual well being of your home, take that position very seriously.

For Moms Especially
If you are a mom, you need to be a strong but not a domineering voice in your home. Allow your kids to see that you

have opinions and the power to discipline and guide them. Allow your kids to see the true meaning of biblical submission: It's respectful support, not an excuse to be treated badly by the man of the house. Let your children see that you are willing to stick by your husband. Show them that you will do whatever it takes to see your husband and children succeed, that you are working for their best interests. Be an advocate for them in the home, in the school, and elsewhere. Help your kids work through the pressures and urges about sex and don't let them run rampant in the house.

Let your daughter see that you love and respect her dad. Kiss and hug your husband in loving and respectful ways, and let her see it. Empower your daughter to make good decisions about choosing friends. Tell her not to fully trust a man right away, that though she may feel love, she should take things slow. Also tell her that no man has a right to her body outside marriage. If there are boys demanding sex as an example of your daughter's love, tell her that it is not really love but cruel selfishness.

Tell your daughter she must guard herself from risky situations. Explain what types of situations are risky. Show your daughter the dangers of dressing scantily and help her find clothes that are appropriate. Tell her that real beauty comes from within, not by what she wears.

Be an open ear to your daughter and let her know that you are willing to help her no matter what, that you will never abandon her even in times of sin and crisis.

If you have a boy, see to it that he respects your voice. You are not a push over. Demand he respects other females in his life. This will become ingrained in his heart if you make him be consistent. Enlist your boy especially in the responsibility of keeping your home in order. Allow him to see that no task is below him or you. Reward jobs well done with praise and love, and laugh and play with your boy. Allow him to feel the full emotion of your heart, no matter what his age, so he will feel free to accept and give that same emotion to his wife.

Talk with your boy openly about sexual issues, relationships, identifying true love, and whatever could get in the way of his sexual purity. Develop a sense of trust and an open door policy if he needs to talk. If you see him making bad decisions, tell him and explain yourself. Make it plain to him that you have a deep love for God, and that you are fully convinced of your relationship with Him. Provide him with a surety of your love.

It Is Possible

I don't claim to have all the answers. But what I have written here is a part of a comprehensive blue print of building up your children in the way they should go when it comes to sexual purity.

Of course there is much more to parenting than what has been listed here. But this is a good start, and I encourage you act on them so your kids will make healthy decisions about sex. If your children have high self respect and respect for you, they will make decisions accordingly.

Many parents don't know that "having the talk" is not just about words. It is a comprehensive task that requires a lot of patience and dedication on your part. But you love your kids, so you know that it is a worthy effort to start now if you haven't already done so.

Sexual purity is a lifestyle. It is about knowledge, thoughts, words, choices, clothing, entertainment, and love. Sexual pressures are all around your kids, so they need you more than ever. Be that example to them. You are their number one influencer.

The best example you can make is to let Christ be the center of your relationship in your family. If you leave this chapter with no other knowledge, I hope you will remember to pray and study daily for the benefit of your children. Their eternities are in your hands; put them on the right path today.

REFERENCES

Chapter 3:
White, E.G. *Letters to Young Lovers.* Washington D.C.: E.G. White Publications.

Chapter 4:
Centers for Disease Control and Prevention (CDC). Tracking the Hidden Epidemic: Trends in STDs in the United States, 2000. http;//www.cdc.gov/nchstp. Stats_Trends/Trends2000.pdf and CDC, Sexually Transmitted Disease Surveillance, 2001,September 2002. http:///www.cdc.gov/std/stats/2001PDF/Survtext2001.pdf

Centers for Disease Control and Prevention. Sexually Transmitted Disease Surveillance, 2004. Atlanta, GA: U.S. Department of Health and Human Services, September 2005.

American Social Health Association. Sexually Transmitted Diseases In America: How Many Cases and At What Cost? Menlo Park, CA: Kaiser Family Foundation; 1998

Centers for Disease Control and Prevention (CDC). HPV Vaccine Q&A.www.cdc.gov/std/healthcomm/ fact_sheets.htm.

National Cancer Institute.(2006). Human Papillomaviruses and Cancer: Questions and Answers.www.cancer.gov/cancertopics/factsheet/ Risk/print?page=&keyword=.

Workshop Summary: Scientific Evidence on Condom Effectiveness for Sexually Transmitted Disease (STD) Prevention. July 20, 2001. National Institute of Allergy and Infectious Diseases, National Institutes of Health, Department of Health and Human Services. Available at: http://www.niaid.nih.gov/dmid/sdts/ condomreport.pdf.

Chapter 5:
Keroack, Eric. (2003). The Neuroendocrine and Biochemical Basics of Human Sexuality: The Results of Non-Marital Sexual Activity. http://www.absti- nence.net/pdf./conentmgmt/EricKeroackPresentatio n2003.pdf).

Chapter 6:
Brown, Jane. et al. (2006). Sexy Media Matter: Exposure to Sexual Content in Music, Television, and Magazines Predicts Black and White Adolescents' Sexual Behavior. Pediatrics 2006, 117; 1018-1027.

Medved, Michael and Diane, Ph.D Saving Childhood: Protecting Our Children form the National Assault On Innocence, P. 19, Harper Perennial, NY, NY 1998.

Kaiser Family Foundation (2003). Sex on TV: A biennial report of the Kaiser Family Foundation Menlo Park Ca. www.kff.org

Chapter 8:
White, E.G. (1995) *The Adventist Home:* Washington D.C.: E.G. White Publications.

Chapman, Gary. (2005) The Five Love Languages: Chicago, Illinois: Northfield Publishing.

Chapter 9:
Kaiser Family Foundation. (2005) U.S. Teen Sexual Activity. www.kff.org.

White, E.G. (1967). *In Heavenly Places*: Washington D.C.: E.G. White Publications.

White, E.G. (1970). *Conflict and Courage*: Washington D.C.: E.G. White Publications.